Don't Look Down

By

Nikki Nyers

Table of Contents

Dedication

As a writer and mom, I dedicate this book, titled "Don't Look Down," to my dearest daughter Noelle. This is not just a simple expression of love but a heartfelt message filled with motivation, inspiration, and unwavering affection.

Noelle, my love, I hope that one day this book will find its way into your arms when you need it the most. I hope its words bring you solace and grant you a clearer understanding of why there were times when I couldn't always be there by your side. Life's challenges and responsibilities often pull us in different directions, but I hope that through my journey, you will find guidance and a beacon of light to illuminate your path.

My darling daughter, you are my ultimate inspiration. Your mere presence in my life has been a driving force, motivating me to overcome obstacles and become the best version of myself. You have saved me from my doubts and fears, and for that, I am eternally grateful. Being your mother is a blessing beyond words, and I consider myself blessed to have you as my daughter.

Remember, Noelle, that my love for you knows no bounds. It is a love that will endure throughout time, unwavering and constant. Through the ups and downs and the twists and turns of life, I will always be there for you, supporting and cheering you on. You are not alone in the journey of life, my dear, as we navigate the world together.

So, my dearest Noelle, take this book into your heart and let its words be a source of strength whenever you feel lost or discouraged. Let it remind you of the unwavering love and dedication I have for you and the infinite possibilities that await you in life. Know that you can achieve anything you set your mind to, my sweet girl, for you possess a strength within you that is astonishing.

Thank you for being the light of my life, my precious daughter. I am immensely proud of the person you are becoming, and I am excited to witness the incredible journey ahead of you. No matter where life takes us, remember that Mommy loves you forever and always.

Acknowledgements

I would like to express my heartfelt gratitude to my mother. Although our relationship may have been minimal and our words fleeting, I want you to know that I love you deeply. This book serves as my humble apology to you, as I struggled to articulate my feelings in person. Your unconditional love and sacrifices have shaped me into the person I am today. Thank you for everything you have done for me since I was little.

To my sister, a guardian angel on earth who possesses nurturing qualities that I have always found comforting and admirable, I want to express my love and appreciation to you. Your unwavering support and understanding have been a source of strength in my life.

To my brother, although there may have been words left unsaid, I hold onto the hope that one day we will find a way to reconnect. I cherish the memories we shared and the bond we once had. I hope that time will heal the wounds and bring us back together.

I am eternally grateful to God, the guiding force in my life. In the beginning, I was lost, confused, and filled with anger. I found myself trapped in the deepest, darkest hole, devoid of light and hope. Each day felt like a struggle, a life I dreaded. It was a path paved with self-destruction, abuse, and depression, as I made terrible choices and mistakes to numb the pain, thank you God, for granting me a second chance at life.

Little did I know that, in time, this journey of despair would lead me towards healing and self-awakening. I had to be lost in order to be found. I had to gather the broken pieces of my life, not only to put them back together but to create an entirely new picture. It was through these shattered fragments that I discovered a greater sense of self and a newfound appreciation for the masterpiece that I have become.

I am forever grateful for the lessons learned and the strength gained from the men who found their way into my heart, only to break it. You have inadvertently bestowed upon me the greatest gift of all: empowerment. Your presence in my life has fueled my passion for music, inspiring me to create and share my art with the world.

Lastly, I would like to express my sincere gratitude to the countless individuals who have supported me throughout my journey. To my talented photographers, my dedicated writing team, and everyone who has played a role in bringing this project to life, I am indebted to your expertise and unwavering commitment.

My ultimate goal with this project is to inspire others in their times of need. I want to convey a message of hope—that even in the darkest tunnels of our lives, a glimmer of light exists. I want to reassure my readers that there is a purpose behind the unexplained and unexpected moments we encounter. God has a plan for us all, and through resilience and determination, we can rebuild our lives and find solace in the healing power of time. "If you can dream it, you can achieve it"

Once again, thank you to every person who has played a part in my journey. Your support and encouragement have made all the difference.

Chapter One
The Beginning Is Always Beautiful

Coley. That's what my family affectionately called me growing up. The year was September 24,1987.The day I was born. My parents welcomed a baby girl into their lives. I was born in Beacon, New York. They named me Nicole Christina D'Alba. My friends always called me Nikki. That is until another girl came to our school and her name was Nicole too. From that point on I wanted to change my name. We moved to California when I was two years old. My parents, brother, and myself. My dad got a job with the police force in San Jose, California. We lived in Tracy, California. My dad worked from 7am-7pm. My mom stayed home to take care of us. I was a tomboy growing up. My parents couldn't keep me inside the house. Whether it was rollerblading, bike riding, water gun fights, or playing basketball with the neighborhood boys. I was an active kid. I loved basketball! I even played basketball for my elementary school. I was unlike the other girls in my neighborhood. That didn't really bother me much. I knew that there was something special and unique about me. I couldn't identify it at an early age. But, I knew there was something about me that made me different from everyone else.

You don't get to choose the family that you are born into in this life.

You become a member of a family and adjust to the people around you. From an early age I knew my family was unlike any other family on our block. For a while that was okay with me. As a kid you don't really have any expectations of the people in your family. I loved my family! They were enough for me. I understood from an early age that there weren't any perfect people in this world. Just imperfect people trying to make the most of the hand they were dealt.

From the time we're born we inevitably accept and love our parents.

My mom and I had a bond that was more solid than peanut butter and jelly.

She was my best friend and confidante in many ways growing up. I knew she loved me but affection was never really shown in our household. It was foreign to me. We knew we loved one another but it was shown in other ways. The words"I love you" were rarely said as it was assumed to be true. To this day I know I longed for that my whole life. I longed to be like other families who said I love you all the time and would seal it with a hug or kiss. However mothers love for us was limitless as she worked endlessly to nurture and support our family. There were days that she wore her weary bones into the ground. I would look at her with empathy brewing inside my heart. I would make promises to myself to give her a better life someday. A life where she would smile more than she cried. A life where her days would be spent basking in the sunlight. Not a day would go by that my mother would want for anything else in this life. I wanted to give her the world and more. If only she would let me, isn't that what we all hope to give our moms?

My relationship with my dad was different. He was the leader and provider of our family. He made sure we all knew it. Our relationship was different from the other children. Most days he'd come home to us broken emotionally and physically drained from the day. He'd bury his sorrow inside a glass of wine and beer. I needed a part of him that I couldn't easily verbalize at a young age. I needed him to be my dad. The guy I built up in my mind as my personal superhero. My protector. My everything. As I grew older I would soon come to know my father as the monster that lived outside my nightmares.

Our siblings are like the extra layer of icing on your birthday cake. You love cake! Too much icing can make you sick. You learn to accept things as they are in your life. In the beginning things in my life were good.

We were a family that lived in a modestly nice neighborhood in a cul de sac in Tracy. I was born the oldest child out of three children. The pressure was on to live up to my parents' high standards of being the perfect child. Not sure if I'd ever measure up in their eyes. I knew I always wanted to make my parents proud of me in some way.

As I look back on my life there were glimpses of memories that I try to hold onto as I grew older. I hold the good stuff near my heart. Right next to the love I have for myself and child. Just to remind me that although the bad times did occur. In between those times there were moments where I really felt alive. I never want to forget all of the things I've been through because without it. I wouldn't know how to appreciate my present. This isn't a rags to riches story or a tell all to get rich quick. I decided to write this book because I understand the power of owning your story and embracing where this journey of life will take you. Along the way some moments will shock your system. While other moments will make you wonder how I made it to see this day. Sometimes I don't even know the answer. I figure as long as I'm living I might as well enjoy the view.

Chapter Two
Suddenly Everything Changes

I don't remember the exact moment my dad decided to move our family across the country. We weren't the type of family to have meetings in our living room over hot coco. Wrong family. Those families only existed in movies as far as I knew. My dad usually made the decisions and the family adjusted. When we moved I was two years old. I was a fairly happy kid. Life was much simpler at this time. I presume little memories young on were better than the disturbing ones I've grasped onto as I grew up.

When I was growing up the only thing that mattered in my world were my extracurricular activities and friends. I was a born dancer. I could feel the rhythm of music in my feet and ripple through my bones. Dancing was just a part of my natural being as a child. It didn't matter the form of dance, I excelled. Ballet,lyrical, jazz, contemporary and etc. I would just come alive on stage. It made my heart smile a mile a minute as I stared back at my mom sitting in the audience at my recitals. Her eyes would get moist as she clutched her hands tightly inside her lap. Her smile said everything she couldn't find the words to speak. She was proud of me. I was her baby girl and I was making her heart smile. It was a magical moment that I would always treasure. The way I felt on stage was incomparable to any other act that would occur in my home life. On stage I was more than just Coley the tomboy or the big sister. I was just Coley the beautiful dancer. My mother was a ballet dancer as well in which we shared a mutual love and bonding. Music was my language that I could speak through movement. Peace sorrow my eloquent choreography would always speak for itself. I loved that part of myself because it gave me the freedom to express myself without limits or negativity. On stage I could float into the air and escape from the harsh things would succumb to my world.

One by one we packed our valuables into a box and large garbage bags. Whatever we couldn't take with us we gave away or left behind. A new life awaited us on the other side of the country. I was excited to start over in a new place. The possibilities were endless. Little did I know that my life would be changed forever.

Growing up as a kid you begin to see things. Things that your young mind may not be able to completely process. Early on in my childhood I was always intuitive and smart. I could often feel the energies of other people. I guess you would say I was very intuitive along with being an empath. Whether that person was good or bad is indifferent. I just knew what my gut instinct would tell me. After my family and I settled in Tracy, California things began to change slowly.My dad got a job in San Jose, California. He worked from 7am-7pm.   My mom was our caretaker. My dad was always working. It got to the point where we rarely saw him. My mom made sure that we were prepared for school. She was very active in our lives early on. She took us to the park often. Somehow we were never that poised and hopeful picturesque family with a growing family we were known for. Suddenly we'd shifted into a family of unfamiliar people that lived underneath one roof. I began to become empathetic to how my mother and siblings were processing our lives in California. That instinctive protective side of me often appeared it's ugly head in me. I was the older sister. It was my job to stand up for what was right. Even in the times I didn't really know how to. I knew there was a part of me that wanted peace, harmony, and comfort always. I desired it constantly as we began our new life in California.

I would stare at my father with curiosity in my eyes. He was the monster in my dreams in the flesh staring back at me. We began to love and fear his presence in our lives. It was weird to think that our lives were shaped by the decisions and actions of my father. He loved us. This I truly believed. But, his addiction to alcohol poisoned his thoughts daily. He began to reign terror over our household. There was not much any of us could do. We were trapped inside the walls of our makeshift castle. As the days would begin to turn to night I became fearful of my father. My resentment began to grow early on within the pit of my stomach. My superhero was beginning to fade before my eyes. All my love that I had within my heart was torn layer by layer with every horrible incident within our home. The verbal abuse, physical. I was know longer daddy's little girl. I was a young girl terrified of the raging alcoholic who slept in the bedroom adjacent to mine. Many nights I'd awake startled inside my bed clenching the sheets. My ears pierced by the sound of my parents arguing on the floor beneath me. They were loud. Loud enough to cause my heart to rattle inside my chest. I remember being so frightened that I could hardly move. That's when I learned that fear was not just something within my imagination. I was afraid. I was afraid to speak up and do anything. I was conflicted at an early age. I wanted to save my mother. I knew she didn't deserve the way my father treated her. She loved him despite his flaws. She loved him when it was impossible to love another human. As time would go on I would watch that light of sunshine begin to wilt away. She was just a woman that loved a man in many ways. But, that man that she committed her life to was long gone. In his place, was a shell of the man he used to be. I promised myself that I would not let him destroy the family we had left. My mother needed us. I needed my mother, We both needed each other in different ways. To this day it's something I long for and struggle to cope with. An emotional emptiness left unhealed.

My dad worked as a patrol cop for the local police department. He protected and served the communities in our area daily. He'd put his life on the line for a stranger during the day. I often felt as if his uniform made him feel invincible. People needed him all over the city. He prided himself on being dutiful to his country. When he came home to his family I could see how the stress of it all wore on his mind. My father wasn't quite the open book when it came to sharing his feelings. He grew up in an old school. Men were to be respected and revered in the home. Women and children were responsible for staying out of sight and quiet. There were days where I wanted to swipe the glass of wine or beer can out of his hand. He'd walk inside the house and sit in his reclining chair. He'd flip through the channels and pour his wine. He was comfortable. Within five to ten minutes of him being home I needed a part of him that I didn't see often . I needed that fun , jovial , playful side , and quirky side to come out. Even for just a moment to listen to me rant on and on about my day. I wanted the kind of relationship with my dad that they model tv families on. Those dads were always present, lively, and easy going guys that loved and adored their families. I began to fall in love with tv shows like Step By Step, Full House, or Family Matters and began to admire the connections or family depiction as I watched in envy. As I grew older I began to realize those sort of families existed only on television or outside our house.

Whenever my parents would argue I would try to cover my ears. It never worked. I could still hear and feel the rage inside their voices. So many harsh colorful words they would spew at each other. Their faces are a different shade of red. Their once toothy grin and puppy dog eyes replaced with disgust and pain. In those moments, it didn't matter who was wrong or right, I wanted my parents to just go back to being normal.

Every so often I sneak outside my room and peek my head downstairs. I'm not sure if I was just being curious or wanting to be a distraction. My dad would see me and demand I go back to bed. I'd run back to my bed and hide underneath the covers. Most nights I found it hard to sleep inside my bed. Most nights if you owned my door you would always find me at the foot of the bed wrapped inside the covers or in my closet. The next day at school I would be very sluggish and tired. My friends would ask what's wrong. I'd blame everything on my siblings or late night television. I couldn't tell people or my friends that my parents kept me up all night arguing. Although I'm sure my friends' parents argue too. I didn't want people knowing our business. I knew the consequences of opening your mouth to the wrong people. I loved my family. I was protective of my mother and siblings. I didn't want anything to happen to any of us. I wanted nothing but peace. When I was little I remember my mother asking me what color paint and blinds I wanted for my room. I chose pink. Pink was always a bright color it made me happy. One day I locked myself in my room with black paint and painted a big peace sign above my desk by my bed as big as could be. A picture is always worth a thousand words. I was trying to get a message out. A silent one in fact. In hopes my dad would come in my room one day, see it and change his ways. But time told that it would be nothing but a wish, a book with an imperfect end. I knew early on that my mother sublingual and I needed to stick together to survive. Even if it meant losing a part of ourselves that we would never get back. We were all we had to fight against my dad.

Chapter Three
The Other Woman Makes Three

I don't remember my exact age when I learned about my father's mistress. However I remember trios to school with our shared van with our father smelling like perfume… but my mom never wore perfume. I overheard the conversation between my parents. It was an argument. My mom had her suspicions that my father was having an affair. He was different. He was not the man she once knew and loved deeply. His drinking had begun to drive a wedge within their marriage. Too many times my father was verbally abusive to my mother. The verbal abuse would often lead to physical abuse. She would try to avoid the abuse by pouring his alcohol down the drain. The abuse would go on for many nights. One of the reasons for their arguments was that my mom alleged that my father was having an affair. My mother did her best to maintain the thread of our family together. She would often hide the pain within her spirit behind her eyes. Know matter what she tried to make us believe that everything would be okay. I began to notice that our once tight knit family was coming unraveled. Our foundation was crumbling each day. I didn't understand what exactly an affair was at the time. I was too young to process the level of impact of my father's choices. I just knew that my mom began to wear a mask figuratively. She would smile and ask us about our day at school. We would be happy to see her each day after school. She tried her best to protect us from the things that our father caused in our lives. Square peanut butter and jelly sandwiches greeted our anxious bellies at the end of the school day. Or trips to The House of Fabrics to do art class in order to maintain a sense of normality within the household. In my eyes she was everything. Our relationship was solidified in my heart from an early age. I never wanted to lose the love of my mother. I could feel my desire to protect my mother grow each time I would feel my fathers' uncontrollable rage. My mom didn't deserve that pain. She was just as innocent as we were in the house.

The other woman was a police officer on the force. She worked closely with my father. There had been signs of an affair earley on. My mother would smell perfume inside the van they shared. Somehow along them being colleagues things began to change. Lines were crossed. Boundaries know longer exist. We were the casualties of my fathers growing desire to feel loved. *Didn't he know my mother loved him? Was her love not good enough? Were we not good enough as a family?*

The affair crushed my mother's spirit. A part of her as a woman was broken inevitably. She was not the same when the affair was confirmed. The spark began to dim inside her eyes. She began to scramble to figure things out for us. Her heart was wounded. My mother's primary role in our lives was the homemaker. She made home as peaceful as possible. Yet, our picture perfect family had cracks in it. Everything was about to change for our family.

Once my mother knew about the affair her behaviour began to change.

One night she pulled us out of the bed and insisted we get in the backseat. She began driving and was eerily quiet. We didn't know exactly where we were going or why. We were following our mothers instructions with sleep inside our eyes. I tried my best to comfort my siblings. They were scared. I could see it inside their eyes. I held their hands and promised them everything would be okay. I whispered to them cautiously. I didn't know if it would. I was just as nervous and scared as they were. I buckled my seatbelt and watched my mother drive down the street. I recognized a few of the houses some close to our school. We pulled into the driveway of an unknown house. But the nightly trips on this path became frequent. My mother was frozen in place as she sat behind the steering wheel. The headlights from the car bounced off the dark house. We sat inside the car quietly. I could not comfort my mother at this moment. I was just a child. I knew the pain in her heart was something I hoped to never experience as a woman. Tears began to crawl down her cheek. She needed answers. She deserved peace. Her world had been imploded by another woman and the absence of her beloved. We sat with my mother in her pain inside the car. I learned that this wasn't just any house on the block. This was the home of the woman who my father wanted a new beginning. His old family was no longer good enough in his eyes. He was unhappy within the walls of terror that he created in our home. I didn't know the feeling of hate or disgust. I discovered it within that moment for my father. My resentment had shifted to hate within a short period of time. I couldn't understand how he could do this to his own family. In many ways I felt violated and broken. He abandoned the family when we needed him the most. A hole in my heart grew exponentially that night. We'd drive by the other woman's house frequently. We knew my father was inside. Somedays his car was in the driveway. He'd made his decision to separate from us. I felt the

uneasiness of my mother's love for a man resting on my shoulders. Her loving heart couldn't quite process her new reality. She married for the promise of happily ever after. Suddenly, she was wrapped up in a nightmare that was beginning to rip through our entire family. I'd made up my mind that I was done with my father. Just as he was done with our family. He was not welcomed in my life anymore.

Chapter Four
Everything Changes Eventually

My parents divorced when I was in the first grade. The affair was more than my mother could deal with in our home. Before I knew it we were living apart from my father. But yet we would have weekly visitations with him in his car while he read us books. No one ever sat us down and told us what was happening within our family. We just learned to adjust to the things happening around us. One incident that sticks out in my mind is the Christmas before my parents got divorced. My dad had stopped by the house to bring us gifts. We were excited to see him. His visit wasn't very long. Just as quickly as he had arrived. He was ready to leave. We were in the living room begging my father to stay. He had gotten us remote controlled race cars. Yet sober, he left just as quickly as he came. Never did I know that these were the memories of my childhood that I would clasp on to the most. My father had decided that he wanted to spend the holiday with his girlfriend.

I think that was hard for my mother to swallow. I assume that because it was the holidays she hoped maybe my father would come to his senses. Be with his family the way they always imagined. But, my father was committed to starting his life over with his girlfriend. There was nothing we could do to change his mind. The marriage was over.

After a while my mother found the courage to leave. The first apartment was a three bedroom. My sister and I shared a room. My brother had his own room. My mom had a room. Financially my mom couldn't afford the three bedroom. My dad was not contributing to the finances. Thus, we were forced to downsize into a two bedroom apartment. My mom had her own room and we shared the other room. Our home we shared with my father on Yorkshire Loop went up for sale.

This was our starter home in California. Back when everything seemed normal, my mom decorated our first house nicely. She put her special touches on the house to make it feel like home. When we moved out of the house on Yorkshire Loop the home was destroyed. My father had punched holes in the wall. The staircase was loose because my father had shook it many times during his drunken stupor. The home was kept and purchased by our fathers new girlfriend. My dad's girlfriend maintained her position on the police force. We were able to keep our old rooms. I remember vividly telling her that her new room could be the closet upstairs. I immediately hated this woman who was to blame for my family being torn apart. We had to make an adjustment to a new member of the household. Although we were back in the house, not much had changed. My father's old patterns and self destructive behaviour reemerged. He began drinking excessively. One wine glass would lead to another. He would start an argument with us, the kids, or with his girlfriend. We didn't know if it was the stress from the divorce or work that was bothering him. It always led to us being a target. It became an uncomfortable environment to live under the same roof. I would always have a distress feeling in my stomach. My parents had a split visitation between my mom and dad. When the school days ended my father would pick us up from school I knew I didn't want to go home with him. I knew what things would lead to at his house. There was always a problem in the home. Whether it was a financial burden or court to finalize the divorce. It was all being taken out on us. I hated packing my belongings every few days to switch households along while my mom awakening us early to drop us off at my fathers house at 4:00am so she could commute to work. Sleep was something my siblings and I desired as I found it hard to stay awake in class. It was an uncomfortable environment for us all.

My mom was beginning to stand on her own two feet. She began working long hours. She would wake us up at four in the morning. She would drop us off at our dads place so he could take us to school in the morning. My mother would have a long commute to work. Although she was working hard, money was still tight. We would collect recyclables for extra money. We didn't have a lot of time with my mom. We made the best of the time we shared together. She was the normal parent sortaspeak. She realized early on that she had a lot of responsibility on her shoulders. She was stressed often.

As I began to grow older I began to become more terrified of my father's verbal abuse. Sometimes it became physical with my dad. This abuse went on for many years. It was terrifying to even get in the car with him. Sometimes my dad would drive drunk. The police were always at our home. My dad would be so intoxicated sometimes that he would start these home projects. Projects that he would never finish. Whether it was ripping out the carpet, he had plans for us to get new flooring. But, we had such a broken home that we didn't have actual furniture. Our couch was an actual van seat. For the longest time, we didn't have a water heater because my dad couldn't afford to get it fixed. We would take cold showers for a long time. There were holes in the walls covered by wallpaper that we used to erase the memories. He would leave the oven door open when we would come down for breakfast because he couldn't afford to turn on the heat. Accompanied by holes in doors due to my father's raging fist. It never felt like home anymore. The loving home that my mom had created no longer existed. This was the home we lived in with my dad. It was not comforting for me.

My father's girlfriend was very nice to me and my siblings. Although I resented her we did spend much time with her so coexistence became easier with time. After a while she became fed up with my fathers drinking and abuse. I always felt like the protector of my siblings growing up. My love for them was unconditional and limitless. We would go to counseling during the divorce proceedings. We would have to draw pictures of how we were feeling. I was always terrified of letting people know exactly how I felt inside. I was afraid of voicing the issues that were bothering me. I knew that things would get back to my dad. I knew on some level that it would make things twice as worse for me and my siblings. I knew we would have to go back to my dad's house at some point.

The counseling sessions lasted for a good while during the divorce. I know my parents were trying to do what was possibly best for us. But, it was torturous to be put in the middle of a divorce. During family dinners at my grandmother's house my father would drink too much. We all knew that it was a matter of time before things would get bad. My father's drinking would often lead to an uproar at home. The next day at school would be challenging to function properly. There was so much to process at a young age that I could feel myself shutting down. My friends would be a place of peace. For me school was an escape of the reality I had to deal with at home. I would go over to my girlfriends house. It seemed like they had everything. It was normal over there. I remember walking through my friends house and recognizing there were no holes. No holes in the wall or doors. That was the life I wanted for myself. Yet deep down I always wished I had a home like theirs to invite them over too. Sleepovers or birthday parties were non existent there.

For the longest time I began to wish the worst upon my father. I would wish that he would die. I even thought being taken away was a better option.I wished the worst upon him all the time. I knew my thoughts were unhealthy. But, the way I was feeling on the inside was heavy and confusing. I just wanted to feel a sense of belonging in the world. I began to carry the weight of everything on the inside. I didn't feel safe or comfortable opening up to many people about my life. I just felt as if there was no one who could save me. I felt hopeless.

Chapter Five
Growing Up In Pain

I was entering my first year of high school. My freshman year I became heavily addicted to drugs. It was an escape from my reality. I began drinking and partying frequently. I left home. My mom was a peacekeeper in the family. However, with her demanding work schedule after a while she couldn't control anything. She had no other choice but to let me go. I believe that is the reason why we had a difficulty developing a close bond. We were much closer when I was a kid. Yet, as I grew older my relationship with my mother began to suffer. I began to place the blame on both my parents for my turnout and failures. I left home around the age of fifteen or sixteen. I moved into a room at my friend's place. I had my own room. I paid rent. I had two jobs. I worked as a hostess at a restaurant and at a kiosk in the mall. I was proud of the home I lived in. A place I deemed a safe haven with nothing my dad could destroy. My life began to evolve around working and being in school. Although I was beginning to learn to take care of myself and gain my independence. The stress of being able to support myself weighed heavy on me. I was running from the thought of having to go back to living with my dad. I continued to do the things that I thought would make me happy. Drinking and doing drugs became a part of my everyday life. The drugs and drinking gave me a temporary high. In my mind this was the temporary happiness I needed to escape from home.

My family knew what I was doing at my friends house. It wasn't long before my dad found out. With my dad being a cop he was trained to recognize the signs of a drug user. I blamed my erratic behaviour on him. I felt like I didn't have a choice because of my home life. I knew my choices were unhealthy and leading me down a destructive path. I had come to the conclusion that drugs and alcohol were a part of my life now. This is what my life has come too. My relationship with my mom became more strained and distant. I barely spoke with my dad. I became more resentful of my father because of the way he treated me and my siblings. Even though he was going through stress at that time. It was no excuse to make his children suffer. I hated him with a passion. I wished the worst on him. I was determined to live at my friends place for as long as possible. I didn't want to return to the hell that we lived in.

One particular day I decided to speak out to my mom. I don't know if I was just fed up or tired from dealing with everything on my own. Something inside of me broke. I was done holding things inside. I knew telling my mom about everything happening at my dad's house was risky. I wasn't sure what her response was going to be. I just knew I had to release what was holding me back in my life. I called my mom before I went into class that morning. By noon, I received a phone call that the police were on the way to my dad's house. My mom was having my siblings removed from my dad's house immediately. My parents still had split visitation. With the police supervision, we grabbed our things quickly. We were escorted to my moms house permanently. At this point in my dad's life he was single. Living in a 2 bedroom apartment. While his bed became his recliner that he rocked himself to a drunken peaceful sleep at night. His girlfriend had left due to the stress and excessive drinking anymore. She was a smart woman. I felt for her immensely because she thought my dad would start over with a new family. He promised her a better life. I remember her flipping through bridal magazines while she chain smoked her cigarettes and sipped her coffee asking which dresses I liked. At some point she had concluded that she was just our babysitter. The life she envisioned was slowly slipping through her hands.

It was a while before my mom caught on to my addiction and erratic behaviour. I was too deep into my addiction by this point. I knew she couldn't do anything about it. I was resentful to both of my parents. I desired a normal childhood. I wanted to be normal like my friends. I wanted to have friends come over to my home and hang out. The reality of coming from a broken home at my dad's house always prevented that. I was proud of the house I lived in with my friends. We had furniture and the basic essentials to make it feel like home. It was a big contrast to being in my father's house with him destroying everything in the house. I drifted from my mother too far from repair from my actions so her home was not an option.

Early on during the transition before my move out I remember my dad's girlfriend attempted to cover the holes in the wall with wallpaper. She tried her best to normalize the home. It was almost an impossible battle to win. I needed that love, nurturing, and secure presence in my life. My mom was very good at providing this sense of love and support in small doses. Our relationship was good better that descent before my entry to high school.

She would take us on vacation to South Carolina where my grandparents resided. My grandparents are amazing people. They are believers in Christ. They did a lot to contribute to our lives in a positive way. They helped my mom relocate out of the two bedroom apartment and into a townhouse. With my grandparents' support, my mom found it easier to stand on her two feet. I needed that love, affection, and positivity in my life growing up. I was happy to receive it whenever I could from the people that loved me. I began to notice that I was becoming codependent on needing love and affection from other people. I began to seek relationships to fulfill the void in my life. I wanted to be loved. I jumped into a relationship early on in my life. During the years of addiction I recall getting pregnant early on.My grandparents didn't know anything about my pregnancy. They still don't to this day. It's something I struggle to cope with or find the words to explain. I began to hate myself for my actions. My mom and dad found out. I confided in my sister and a few close girlfriends. My friends always had my best interest in mind. Even though I had their support, I realized I couldn't take care of myself. I was very young. I didn't realize the repercussions my choices would have on me in life. Looking back on all of my poor choices I realize I was searching for a part of myself. When you're looking for a part of yourself you're bound to make some mistakes. My friends helped me to locate an abortion clinic in Stockton, California. During the drive to the clinic I didn't know what to expect. My friends did their best to comfort and reassure me I was doing the right thing. I knew I wasn't ready to be a parent. I could barely support myself. I was fifteen. Bringing a baby into my life was a responsibility that I knew I wasn't prepared to take on. As scared as I was, I was grateful to have the support of my friends. I could feel my heart skipping rapidly as we approached the abortion clinic. My feet were moving towards the door as I tried to wrap my brain around what I was about to do. I wasn't a very spiritual or religious person growing up. I knew God existed. He'd saved me quite a few times in the past. I knew I needed to call on him to save me this time. I needed as much support as possible to move forward. I knew someday I would have to ask for forgiveness. Forgiveness for ending a life so soon. Forgiveness for choosing an alternative option. Forgiveness for my own mistakes and poor choices. Today, I needed forgiveness from God first. I would have regret and disgust in myself for a long time.

By the time I woke up I was surrounded by women. The nurses provided me with juice and cookies to raise my blood sugar. The pain from the abortion was more than I handle. The person whom I was in an intimate relationship with at the time was not emotionally available. I could see the expression on his face clearly. He was not remorseful or sad in any way. He began to withdraw from the relationship. I discovered that he was dating someone else. I was just someone he chose to spend his in between time with at the moment. I wasn't aware of whether are not our relationship was evolving into something more or not. I guess I was just in a place where I wanted to be in companionship. It didn't matter if that companionship led to a bright future. He was just the person that I was choosing to love in this particular chapter of my life. I guess I could say I was in love with him in some way. Over time I had established a strong emotional connection with this person. I hoped that it was a two way street. It wasn't. I had to learn that people don't love you the way you want them too. They can only love you in the capacity of loving themselves. It was a hard lesson. But , it was a lesson that I needed to learn early on in my life.

Chapter Six
Growing Up Fast

When my mom found out about the abortion she was very upset with me. It wasn't long before my dad found out. I was not in a good place to accept their words of why my life was such a train wreck. My relationship with my dad was so strained at this point. Him being disappointed in me was a major factor in my life. I had built up such a disdain for my father that I had become numb to being in his presence. My heart was cold and hard as a rock towards my father. He was the last person that I wanted advice from about life. To a certain extent, it mattered what my mom thought about me.

I knew she didn't deserve another disappointment in her life. I knew she had high hopes for all of her children. Myself included.

I wanted to make my mom happy. But I was so far into my addiction that her heartfelt words would fall on deaf ears. I was ready to move on from the situation without everyone's opinion on my life. Everything inside of me was telling me that I was smart enough to figure things out. I was making things happen for myself without my parents in my face. I didn't need their permission to live my life the way I wanted.

I became involved in another relationship. I was living with my friends at the time. I was looking for a fresh start on life. I wanted to start doing better in my life. I knew that I needed to improve my grades. For so long I had squandered most of my high school academics on my addiction. I had become accustomed to not being fully present in class. I used to skip school just to go get high. My senior year of high school was approaching fast. I was in dance classes and the dance team. Those brief moments of being on the dance floor and feeling the rhythm of the music. Flowing through my body allowed me to wake up every fiber of my being. I wanted to always feel that euphoric feeling as long as I was alive. My life was never that simple. That high that brought me to life on the dance floor was often found in a powder for me. It wasn't long that dance would become a emotional memory I identified with as that was stripped from me too as I was kicked off the dance team and taken out of my dance classes altogether. I participated in dance class five days a week for an hour sometimes two a day. Between the high school dance team and the hometown studio I attended to for 7 years. Dance superseded school as I had to always make time for working at night. But my juggling act would come to an end as I felt like the clown who squandered their grades away.

Once my grades started to fall significantly, I had to leave the dance team. Leaving the dance team was perhaps the most difficult part of my high school experience. Dance was the only thing in my life that didn't judge or ridicule me. Dance was always there to welcome me back with an open hand. For so long dance had become an intricate part of my life that I couldn't see a future without it. My proudest moments were in dance being at the recital performing. I could see the smiling faces of my family and friends looking back at me. They were all so proud of Coley. They believed in the magic of my dreamers as a dancer. They could see me, just as me. I realized from an early age that dance was something my mom and I shared. She was once a dancer at a time in her life. We bonded over our love of dance. Dance was the one thing in my life that I excelled in and wanted to hold on to forever. Suddenly, all of that and more were beginning to slip through my fingers because of my addiction.

A teacher I had in my senior year allowed me to find a safe haven in our budding friendship. I began to open up to her about my life and the things I was constantly battling. I even told her about my addiction and how I had lost my focus in school. There was something special about our relationship because many people would have not cared about me. Some people would have judged me for my poor decisions and betrayed my trust. This particular teacher was like an angel from heaven. Instead of ridiculing me, she opened her heart and provided a safe space for me. She bore the nurturing aspects of a mother which I needed the most at the time. At last someone who understood me. I'd never had an adult come into my life and assure me that it was okay that I wasn't perfect. Most people just wrote me off as a troublemaker or troubled child that was difficult to love. One of my closest friends even told me her mother said we weren't allowed to hang out anymore because I was deemed to be a bad influence. It hurt, the pain compiled but deep down I knew my character to be true at heart. I did agree now that my actions were not the best in which I would now say the same thing as a mother of a poor friendship. I was able to talk about my family and the things we were facing with this teacher. She really connected with me on a human level. She was compassionate and down to earth as much as possible. I could see that I had struck a chord in her heart as well. She began champing me to take control over my life again. She pushed me towards getting my grades on track. She helped me pass her class during my senior year. I don't know if it wasn't for her help I wouldn't have made it. I passed. I graduated from high school. My family was extremely proud of me. My mom was at my graduation. Even though I graduated, I knew I would always be upset that I had to give up dance.

Once I lost my main job as a hostess at a local restaurant followed by my job at a dealership I was forced to move out of the house I was living in. It forced me to clean up my act quickly set my addiction problems aside and start a new relationship with someone quickly. So quick to where I could live with them and not be forced to return to my past. I moved into the townhouse of the person I began dating. It was a neighbor of my mothers. He was newly single, we shared a mutual fondness for one another and I of course still struggling with codependency. It was perfectly imperfect. Our relationship was pretty serious enough for us to consider living together. Our relationship progressed so quickly that we became engaged. It was a wild and passionate love between us.

Even though he was much older than me I loved him from a genuine place. Our age difference was about ten years. He was more established and mature than me. I tried to not allow the age gap to affect our relationship. I did my best to impress him with my cooking skills and little acts of kindness. I was eager to show the skill set I acquired so early on as I felt forced to identify with the term adulthood early on. I had a different sense of appreciation for life at this time. I had enrolled in college to take on a few courses. I overcame my drug addiction. I would only drink in a quiet setting at home occasionally and not in a social setting to prevent myself from being coaxed down a bad path. This was a new leaf in life for me. I was proud of all of my strides to become a better person. I knew life wasn't ever going to be perfect. I just needed to get to a point in my life where things made sense to me. For most of my life I'd struggled with adjusting to the verbal and physical abuse brought on by my father. As much as I had buried inside of my addiction, there were wounds on my body that couldn't heal. The marks I would leave on my arm to disassociate from the internal pain. Know matter how much time would go by. I was often reminded of the nightmare of my childhood and the gaping hole in my heart searching for a perfect love. I would often come close to peace or something like it. But, I could never feel one hundred percent safe with the direction of my life until I made peace with my upbringing.

Chapter Seven
The Phone Call

I don't remember the exact day and time I received the call. I was job searching when I received a call from my mom. Within a matter of minutes she told me that my dad was in the hospital. I didn't know how to feel in the moment. My mom told me my father wasn't doing well. I remember early on in our childhood that my dad would go to doctors appointments. I had to drive him to a few appointments. He would never be open with us and tell us what's going on. My dad was very quiet about his medical issues. My mom warned me that I could go and see my father. But he wasn't open to seeing me. I almost didn't feel the need to go because of our distant relationship. We were at the point in our father/daughter relationship where we normalized not speaking for months at a time. It had come close to a year where I didn't speak to my dad. Not talking to my dad was a sense of relief for me . I resented him so much that I rationalized that it was okay not talking to him ever again. I know that may seem strange for a child to say about their biological parent. But, my truth was that my father was not the typical American dad that loved and adored his children. I'm sure he loved us in some shape or form. The way he expressed that love to us was traumatic and unforgivable in my eyes. I wanted to make him pay for all those sleepless nights I spent crying in bed to fall asleep. The brutal cold showers before school. Or just coming into a house where an alcoholic is raging mad about anything. I wanted my father to beg for my forgiveness. He owed me that. He owed me a peaceful childhood. He owed me a normal upbringing. He owed me every experience he ever robbed me of being happy. I wanted him to regret losing me out of his life. I wanted retribution.

I decided to drive up to the hospital. It was an hour away from where we lived. My dad's side of the family arrived at the hospital. Everyone was there to support my dad. My dad was admitted into the hospital. Everything began happening so fast. Due to the extent of my dad's drinking and his other health complications. He was diagnosed with cirrhosis of the liver. I broke down crying. For as far back as I could remember I had wished the worst on my dad. I never imagined what I would feel like on the day my words would be true. Growing up I wanted my dad to suffer immensely the way he made us suffer. I wanted to make him regret the way he treated us and feel at least half of that pain. But, I knew the diagnosis was the worst that happened to my dad. Many people had died from cirrhosis of the liver. I never thought my dad would be one of them. I figured we had more time left to figure things out. Work through our differences and repair the relationship. Now everything was in question and we were racing against time.

Chapter Eight
A Long Goodbye

Everything was starting to become a reality for me. My dad was about to leave this earth. His days were numbered. It was hard for me to face the reality that I may never see him again. A small part of me knew that he was my dad and the love was still there. Even if it was dormant at times inside of me I still had some love left for my dad. I just couldn't wrap my mind around the idea of losing my dad. So many emotions started to erupt inside of me all at once. I could barely process everything I was feeling.

Luckily, my aunt and uncle on my dad's side could see I was visibly upset.

They opted to get me a hotel room. The hotel was close to the hospital. Everyone on my dad's side of the family was present in the hospital. We began to take turns visiting my dad. I went into his room to talk to him. The nurses had started to administer morphine. He wasn't conscious of everything happening around him. I did my best to speak with him. I remember sitting in the room and he looked over at me. He asked me, ``Why was I there?" I told him I wanted to be. We talked. I opened up to my dad and let him know that I stopped using drugs. I told him that I desired to dance again. I wanted him to know that I was doing better. I'd even gone so far as to enroll in college.

As I began opening up more to my dad, I began watching him slip away. The morphine was easing some of his discomfort. I had to realize that he may not have understood everything I was saying. But, I knew he could appreciate the fact that I was there right by his side. Nothing else mattered in that moment. I needed to be by my father's side. I don't know if I ever forgave my father for all the things he did to me. I couldn't do it in just one moment. I had to get to a point where my desire for a normal dad or normal childhood was something my dad couldn't give me.

We all began to have our one on one time with my dad. My brother and sister were able to say their last goodbyes. We were all there to hold each other. I remember leaving the hospital in tears. I had broken down in the hallway and started crying. The flood of tears that were covering my face made me realize I wasn't quite ready to say goodbye. Everything was coming up all at once inside of me. I had to come to terms that there wasn't a cure for my dad. He was going to die. Even with everyone surrounding me at seventeen I was still very angry. I was angry about everything and that anger was erupting inside of me. I needed to get out of there. I was feeling horrible because of all the things that were coming up inside of me.

My aunt and uncle tried their best to make everyone comfortable. They suggested we all go out and eat. I didn't have an appetite for anything. We were all gathered in the parking lot. I couldn't pretend like nothing wasn't bothering over hot pizza. The people around me didn't understand the depth of my pain. I started to run towards my car. I ran so fast that my uncle's voice fell on deaf ears. He wanted me to come back and be with the family. Everyone knew my past. They knew all of the things I'd struggled with in my life up until this point. They probably assumed that I was running to go get high. Getting high was the furthest thing from my mind. I drove back to the hotel. I sat inside my hotel room and cried. I cried for what felt like an eternity. I cried until I couldn't cry anymore. I picked up the phone and called my mom. I told my mom that I had spoken to my dad.

I wanted her to know that I had tried to make amends before he passed.

My mom understood my intentions as she tried to comfort me.

Later that night, I was trying to sleep when I was startled awake. It was the middle of the night. Something told me to drive over to the hospital. The urge to go directly to the hospital was very strong. I couldn't deny the feeling. I jumped inside my car and headed directly to the hospital. I ran into my dad's room. The nurses let me in even though it was late at night. I entered my father's room which was shared. Nobody else was in the room with us. I pulled out the cot next to the bed. I moved the cot next to the bed to be close to my dad. I could tell that the morphine had him so far gone that he wasn't conscious of my presence. He was laying in bed making sounds. Sounds of pain. His eyes were yellow. His liver was failing. His skin pale and lifeless.. I just laid next to him and held his hand. I began closely watching the monitor. I couldn't understand what everything meant. His heart rate was beginning to decline. I remember just holding my dad's hand to comfort him. I fell asleep holding his hand. His hand would tighten around mine. There was a final moment of peace that overcame my soul at that present moment. Time stood still as tears soaked the pillow that lied beneath my head. I knew he realized I was there next to him. Another patient needed to enter the room. I had to vacate the room temporarily. I held his hand a little longer. It was late at night when I drove back to my boyfriend's place. I packed an overnight bag and headed over to my mom's. My uncle rang my mom earlier before I got to her house. He reached out to my mom and confirmed that my dad had passed.

Chapter Nine
Starting Over Again

On his deathbed my father made me promise to quit my drug use once and for all. . I promised him I would. However,I felt a sense of resentment and anger upon his passing. I began to resort to drugs, again. It didn't really all hit me until after his passing. My dad gave me a black box for graduation. It was a black box that he sent to me. It was supposed to hold my diploma. I remember being so angry with my dad that I began snorting cocaine off the box. He was gone and the memories began to flood my mind. It was as if a levee had broken inside of me. All of the pain and trauma of everything I went through in my childhood came rushing to the forefront of my mind. I wanted to make the memories go away. Silence the voices inside my head that made me want to crawl inside my skin. I was beginning to sink inside of a dark place that would be impossible to climb out. Cocaine was the first drug that I was exposed to too. It was while I was working in California that I was exposed to drugs. The group of friends I had at that time influenced me a great deal. Somehow I convinced myself that my behaviour was normal. The people around me didn't seem to have a problem with their drug usage. I figured I was just as fine as they were at times.   Cocaine was expensive. Methamphetamine was another drug choice of mine. Ecstasy gave me a euphoric high that I craved. I wasn't proud of my deadly habit at all. It was a part of me. But, it didn't define who I was as a person. Some people coped with sex, alcohol, or pornography, This was my vice. This was something that I would have to fight to overcome in my life.

While living at the house I was still involved with the older man in my life. When he came into my life it was like a lightbulb came on inside my head. I began to really change for the better. I didn't want to continue down this downward spiral of destroying my life, It was like this older man in my life could see through all of my bullshit and help me. He wanted me to become my best self. He wouldn't accept anything less of me. I appreciated him for it. I wanted to be someone that he could be proud of at the end of the day. I appreciated the fact that he was older than me. He had a different perspective on life. His values and morals encouraged me to get on the right path. I wanted him in my life. I knew being with him would require me to be mature and not be a failure. I'd felt like a failure most of my life. I began pushing away my friends. I became the perfect housewife in a way. I got a stable job while continuing my college general education courses.

This older man just wasn't a stranger off the street. He was my mother's neighbor. He knew a lot about my background with my dad growing up. He didn't judge me. He knew that I came into a lump sum of money after the passing of my dad. Due to my drug habit I blew the money irresponsibly. At the time I perceived his helping hand as the love and support I needed to get through rough patches. I was caught up in the love aspect of our relationship and naive at times. I began making some questionable decisions. I purchased a truck for him with the little money my father left me. I even went as far as almost co-signing a loan for his education. He needed me to be another paycheck in the household.

Eventually things began to really hit the fan between us, Child support services located him in California. He'd abandon his responsibilities in Maryland and tried to start over in California. He had a child that I was never aware existed. We were deep into our relationship that I was naive to the things he was doing, He would come home late at night. His text messages would be vague and short. While using his computer to write a paper for class. I came across a hidden file of women. The computer file contained nude images of women. Not just any women, but women that I was introduced to by him or he was in contact with daily for work. I wasn't supposed to find that especially when things were not going well. It was the eye opener I needed to leave once and for all. He was very stern and verbally abusive. Traits similar to my father. He made me feel like I had major problems and issues with the way I was my behaviour. He suggested that I needed to go see a psychologist. The psychologist prescribed me medication. Some of the medication was for anti-schizophrenia. I was not experiencing symptoms at the time. It was not clear to me why I was prescribed that medication. I was led to believe that I was the one with the problem. When I discovered those files I made the decision to leave. I went and looked for a place in Pleasanton. While browsing Craigslist, I responded to an ad for a roommate. It was about an hour drive from where I lived with my ex. I didn't want to move backwards. Moving in with my mom was not an option for me. I replied to the post and we set up an interview with my potential roommate.

It was definitely one of the best decisions I ever made. At the same time I had a good supportive friend. She helped me to get a job in the area.

She was definitely a stable and reliable friend in my life from childhood. She was never into drugs or anything like that. She was one of the few people I felt comfortable to confide in about my life. I spent a great deal of time at her house while my dad was alive. I obtained a job in the area as a collection agent. I worked for a subprime lender for a bank that helped finance loans for customers with bad credit for vehicles. This was the fresh start in life that I was anxious to begin. For the first time in my life everything seemed to be lining up and working out for me.

I enjoyed living with my roommate. He became my best friend, my confident. He was one of the most amazing people I met in my life. He was an Indian male who worked for a corporation. He graduated from college in Maryland. He had two bedrooms vacant in the house he lived in. We connected right away. He was very laid back. His personality was very calm and confident. Everything about his aura gave me the boost I needed to really take control of my life. I learned a lot from just being around him. He did like to drink and have fun. Although he never over indulged, he was always grounded. There was another roommate that moved into the house. We weren't as close as Kevin and I. The other roommate worked as a security guard in a few towns over. He worked opposite shifts, we rarely saw each other. Despite sharing the space with two men I enjoyed living in the house. I made the room my own. During this time in my life the house represented something stable in my life. At this time my mother and siblings made the decision to move cross country to South Carolina. After my dad passed my mom wanted to be closer to my grandparents. My grandparents lived in South Carolina. My mom felt as though there was no reason for her to stay any longer in California since my dad passed. My dad was know longer a part of our lives. I understood to a certain extent where my mom was coming from. South Carolina would give her the space and clarity she needed to start over and begin again. We all needed that reset. I needed it too.

I remember my mom telling me she was going to make the move.

Everything began happening so fast. I knew I wasn't going to move to South Carolina. I was finally getting my footing going in my life. I had just moved to the area and I loved it. I was feeling quite proud of myself. I made the tough decision to let my family go. At the job I was working I met another interesting person. His name was Sam. We hit it off right away. He was very interested in sports. That was something that intrigued me in a new way. I enjoyed going to the games, especially basketball and baseball. I was a Warriors and A's fan. He was into the industry. He did stats for the game, specifically for the Warriors and Pac Twelve network. Our desks were pretty close to each other in the office. We became fast friends. He knew my mom and siblings were leaving to make the move across the country. During conversation I'd told him that I lived in a new area and that I would be by myself. He definitely helped keep me grounded. He introduced me to his family. That quickly became my life , everything was finally falling into place. My new friends were my roommate , my co-workers, and My boyfriend I began to feel more like an adult. Even though I was working I was still taking college courses. I thought I wanted to be a nurse. This was the ideal dream career that my dad mom's started out on. My family all had some tie to the medical field. My grandfather a Doctor my grandmother a nurse in the working careers. I just thought that was what was in the cards for me. My mom was involved in the medical field. Everything led me to believe that this was what I was supposed to do. I had no sense of direction. I kind of figured since this was the road that my family traveled and was presumably good at, it would be the same road for me. It was in their blood, it must be in mine.

I completed college courses and tried to get all of the prerequisites out of the way. A year passed, I continued to go out with my roommates and Robert, another close friend of mine. He lived nearby and quickly became part of the group. This was my close group of friends. We always hung out over the weekends and ate together. I was definitely a lot closer to the men in my life at this time.

In Pleasanton, I was starting to become unhappy after a year. I felt as though I had this great group of people in my life. I had a nine to five job and I was enrolled in college. I had weekends off and an amazing boyfriend. His family was great to me. They were supportive of our relationship. Life was great on the outside by all accounts. But, I had a nagging feeling that was continuously growing inside of me. Know matter how many times I tried to tell myself that I was happy with the way things were going for me. My mind kept thinking about my mom, even though we weren't close. I was missing out on moments in the lives of the people I loved and cared about including my siblings. I didn't have much money to go to South Carolina. It started to really impact me in a way that was quite unfamiliar to me. I started to feel as if I was living a superficial life while trying to mask my true self. I tried my best to find things to make me happy including people and relationships. I began to realize I needed to do the work and dig deep inside myself. Doing that consisted of facing my past, my hardships, and my relationship with God that was nonexistent. It also included coming to a clear understanding that I didn't have a relationship with myself. I had failed multiple relationships in my life. Whether the relationship was with my dad, myself, or my friends. I even evaluated my relationships with men that I felt I needed to feel good about myself. I had developed a co-dependency of relying on others to fulfill me. I didn't need that anymore.

I knew I was going through a change where I needed to make amends. I needed to make amends with my family and become closer with them. I started to have problems at night when I would return home from work. I remember multiple nights crying myself to sleep. I was crying because I missed my mom and siblings. I missed my friends too. The life I was creating was not enough for me. I started to look at life as a whole and understand where I was putting my values. I didn't want more time to pass where it was similar to my relationship with my dad. Our relationship was not in a good place. I didn't want to allow history to repeat itself in other relationships in my life. I was coming to the realization that I needed to put more emphasis on the relationships with the people I loved. After the passing of my dad, I realized that our relationship could have been something great and wonderful. If only we were dealt a different set of

cards in this life. I refused to allow my relationship with my mom and siblings to suffer because of where I was in my journey. I knew a part of me desired to move across the country. However, I always viewed California as my home. I understood that I was going to have to make tough decisions in order to repair and maintain the relationships with the people in my life. If I didn't decide soon, life would soon decide for me.

My boyfriend and I were beginning to unravel at the seams. Our problems were consistently threatening the solid foundation of our relationship. There was a huge mistake on my behalf in the relationship. I was always looking to have fun and chase moments of temporary gratification. I was often looking for ways to be daring in some formation in my life. I often acted out in this manner to cover the pain I was masking inside of myself. I knew my relationship wasn't the best at the time. We were beginning to have quite a few problems. It was due to me trying to perfect someone else's imperfections and mold them into the person they weren't ready to be. Deep down I realized now that I was trying to project my shortcomings and insecurities onto my partner. I remember running away to Las Vegas for a weekend with another man. My boyfriend did find out. I realized that our relationship would never be the same. The damage It caused was unforgivable in his book. I couldn't blame him for not wanting to forgive me. I could hardly find the strength to forgive myself. It was in those moments that I realized I was self sabotaging my life and relationships. I did this unintentionally to fulfill the numbness and void inside of me. I was a broken woman in many ways. Yet, I portrayed a woman that was eagerly striving to get her life together in a big way. Know matter how hard I tried to overcome and run from my past, it always showed up in different ways to remind me. Remind me that I was still a brokenhearted girl searching for love and security throughout my life.

One of the main support systems I had in California at the time pulled me to the side. We had an open and honest conversation about what went wrong in my relationship. I wasn't quite clear as to why I did cheat on my boyfriend. He didn't deserve that from me. He tried to love me, all of me. Parts of me that I found difficult and impossible to love. The number one thing that I was always afraid of happening to me was being cheated on. I cheated on my partner. I was conscious in my decision to give a part of myself to someone else. I did that to somebody else. I could only imagine the hurt and pain I caused him. I knew that no amount of apologies would be sufficient to the growing pain inside of his heart. I was more disappointed in myself for causing him pain. As much as I desired a relationship, there were parts of me that were not ready to completely love another person.

Immediately after going through a routine check up. I was advised that I had pre cancerous cells developing in my cervix. I had health insurance. I was able to have an elite procedure done where I was put to sleep while a layer of my cervix was removed. . The doctors began to cut the cancerous cells from my cervix. I was scared. I didn't have my boyfriend there to support me, we were not speaking. I wanted my mom there with me. She was in South Carolina. The procedure and lack of support from my family in my time of need put things into perspective for me. I began to understand that life was really precious. I went to my employer and requested a leave of absence. I put all my belongings in storage. I had a sit down conversation with my roommate. . I let him know my plans to go out to South Carolina to be with my family. He informed me that he was planning to move to Los Angeles to attend a business school. He was in the process of obtaining his graduate degree. My other friends were all moving in different directions as well. Life was beginning to happen all around me. I couldn't control what other people were doing or saying at this time. I knew I just needed to adjust with the changes. I realized that this was possibly the best time for me to be closer to my family.Sam, my boyfriend was still in the back of my mind. Even though we were no longer speaking, I still had love for him. I knew I needed to be with my family. My friends were relocating. I knew in my gut I was making the best decision for me.

We all had one last one gathering. It was right before Thanksgiving. This would be my last Thanksgiving in San Francisco with the people I was closest to along with my roommate. We wanted to make it a memorable moment. We passed out food to the homeless at a local church. It was the perfect ending to a new beginning waiting for me in South Carolina. I purchased a one way plane ticket to South Carolina. I phoned my mom to let her know I would be traveling down South for the holidays. California would always be home. A part of me would always want to come back. My heart was in California. The relationships that I formed with very special people would always be near and dear to me. There was one particular relationship that I could not leave California without resolution. I needed to make sure I left California in peace and not pieces. I phoned this particular person to offer up an apology for all that I had done. He was nothing more than kind to me. I knew I would see my friends again. The peace of mind I gave myself was putting all of my belongings in storage. Everything in the storage was a piece of my life. I knew if I left the storage in California I knew I would come back for it. I would be home again. For now, my home was with my family. I boarded the plane to Hilton Head, South Carolina. I boarded the plane and began balling my eyes out. I realized I was leaving everything behind. My friends, my childhood memories, dad, and everything that made up my whole life. It was a bittersweet moment. I moved to California at two years old from New York. The plane ride to California with my siblings and parents came flooding to the forefront of my mind. The move to a new city and meeting Tracy all was coming back to me like a movie. I had lived an interesting life in California. Now I was ready to begin a new chapter.

Chapter Ten
One Family Reunited

When my mom came out to South Carolina with my sister, they drove cross country. They had everything shipped out later. I came out with one suitcase. All of my memorabilia were located in California. My most memorable items were my dad's Thomas Kincaid artwork picture that he had framed. He loved Thomas Kincaid, he was my dad's favorite artist. We had a lot of pictures in the house that were not damaged or destroyed. The artwork was left to me. The belongings got split up after the passing of my dad. He was cremated and put into a box. My mom took some of the ashes while the remainder laid with my grandparents in Las Vegas. My grandparents received some ashes to have a memorable piece of my dad. The rest of his ashes were in a box. My mom hid the box in a china cabinet for a long time.

Once I moved to South Carolina I moved to my mom's house. I moved in as a way to begin to reconcile our relationship. I settled into a room inside her home. I was getting paid for FMLA due to my medical procedure. I had my one suitcase and one of the things

I started doing right away was cooking. I would cook every single night. I wasn't working so I would cook for my mom and siblings. We all lived under my moms roof. Cooking made me happy. It took up time and gave me an opportunity to reflect. Not only that, it was something that my dad often did in our home as a kid. I remember in the middle of the night due to his daily work schedule. The nights my dad were off he would prep his meals. Even during the day when he would try to sleep. My dad would wake up and he would start cooking . The house would smell so good. My dad was really good at cooking. He would even take some of the food to the inmates. They loved his cooking just as much as we did at home. For my dad cooking was like a bonding experience. Maybe my dad got it from his dad's grandad because he also loved to cook. Watching my dad cook was one of the most positive memories of my childhood. When we would go over to my grandparents, my grandparents would make sausage from scratch. He'd have me help or bring me homemade bread. When it was just my grandparents and just us kids they would just watch us in the kitchen trying to cook. Thus, I remember cooking always having the power to connect and heal families.Cooking was something I adopted into my routine and it brought me great joy. I'm sure my mom and siblings enjoyed the home cooked meals.

Shortly after arriving in South Carolina I began looking for a job. When I knew that my pay would stop from FMLA. I phoned my employer to let them know I would not be returning to work. My employer and I parted ways amicably. I found a job in South Carolina at a gym assisting with admin tasks. I worked consistently for a few gyms until I got an opportunity to work in food and beverages. I remember the first few nights going out to eat with my mom and sister at a true southern country restaurant. It was at that very moment my heart sank as I struggled to process my surroundings. This plain lifeless room in a slow trendless country town lacked the California city life that I became accustomed to.An endless stream of tears fell from my cheeks as I sat there losing my appetite. I thought I had regretted my decisions leading up into this point. Everything was a culture shock for me moving to Bluffton, South Carolina. There were not a lot of street lights and the people dressed differently. There wasn't as much judgement in South Carolina compared to California. California is a state where people judge you based on where you are in life and how you present yourself to the world. You try your best to impress everyone and live a superficial life in California. I felt that what I thought that's what California was as a whole. Out in South Carolina it was very different. People are very laid back and polite, just overall different. I didn't know if different was good for me. At times I did feel lonely. Even though I had my family we weren't as close still. A lot to do with our lack of closeness was impart on my decision to leave the house at an early age. There was a deep bond lacking, I knew I wanted to fulfill. I enrolled in college courses in South Carolina with the help of my grandparents. Life was starting to get on track across the country. I can honestly say it was one of the most memorable times where I realized my mom was really proud of me. She never thought I had the courage to make a change move across the country. I graduated with an Associates degree in Art from a local college. I changed my career path even though my primary focus was on nursing. I desired to have multiple degrees before I entered the nursing program. Walking across the stage to get my Associates degree was one of the proudest moments of my life. My grandparents were happy and proud of me. They were happy we were all close to them and doing well. My mom was there and happy for me. I soon received the acceptance letter to enter the nursing program. That was by far the proudest moments of my life. I was starting to feel as though things were finally working out for me . I felt accomplished and excited to embark on the new chapter of my life.

Chapter Eleven
Becoming A Mom

I was pregnant. I stood inside the bathroom holding the pregnancy test for what felt like hours. I couldn't believe my eyes. I didn't know how to feel in the moment. My head was spinning by the second. I was overcome with a sea of uncertainty and anxiety. I wasn't ready to become a mother. I was 27 with little accomplished in life. There were so many more things I wanted to do with my life. Becoming a parent at a young age was not it. I was on the road to reclaiming my life. I had a few stumbling blocks to overcome but I was making things happen for myself. I was in a place in my life where I was still unclear about my purpose in this world. But, I'd given up the fast lifestyle and late nights. I was on a new path. I was trying to understand myself as a woman. That is until, I met someone new. I didn't subscribe to love at first sight. We were more than just a quick fling. We friends and lovers. Our relationship started with fireworks and grew into something serious quickly. Before I knew it, we were serious about each other. He satisfied my needs on more than a basic level as a man. I needed someone to make me feel beautiful and lift up my spirits when I needed it. I wasn't looking for someone to save me. I was saving myself from everything I'd overcome in the past. I knew our relationship had the potential to become everything I was hoping for in a partner.

I was never late. Growing up I had abnormal cycles. It wasn't that unusual for my monthly to be a day or two late. But, when more than a week went by I became concerned. I was nervous about telling (insert guy name) about the possible pregnancy. I knew him well enough that I knew the news would send him sparrolling. I decided to wait. I needed to wrap my head around the possibility of becoming a mom. When I had my abortion as a teenager I was nervous about my parents finding out. I knew I was living wild and uninhibited at the time. Pregnancy was possibly the last thing on my mind. I knew I wasn't ready to accept the consequences of my action. I knew that being pregnant and having a baby would be a major life decision. It was one I didn't want to take for granted. It was the best decision for me at the time.

Now that I'm older it's still quite scary to think about on my own. I watched my mom work night and day to provide for us. I appreciate all of her sacrifices and hard work. I couldn't imagine the tough choices she had to make. But, that's not the road I want to explore with my children. My mom was never really there for me emotionally or physically. She didn't understand all the things that were bothering me while living with my dad. I know she tried her best to be a good mom. But, there are things that she taught me about being a woman and a mom that will live with me forever.

On December 16, 2014, I gave birth to my daughter.She was far far from perfect. Her big blue doe eyes gazed back at me as she was weighed in at 8lbs as I welcomed her into my cradling arms. I was her protector the one human she would forever most become dependent upon. My pregnancy was high risk due to my prior procedures with cervical cancer cells. I worked everday of my pregnancy. It was the most rewarding experience I have ever endured. As I carried my daughter in my tummy for 9 months with swollen feet waiting tables I knew nothing could stop me. I was determined to be the greatest mother she could ever dream of while giving her everything I deeply longed for. She would be the one to heal me with the lord as my savior. I worked with the father of my daughter. I worked on my due date. Noelle's father and I had only been together five months when I got pregnant.

Discovering that I was pregnant at this stage in my life was exciting. This was a blessing for me. I worked every single day including my due date. I was living with Noelle's dad during the pregnancy. We had become best friends. Everything was normal. He prepared my meals and made sure I was comfortable as possible. He made sure I was stress free during my pregnancy. The financial challenges we faced were not a major obstacle for us. I was pretty good with saving my money. I worked to save. I didn't want to put myself in a position to be codependent on him. I broken that spell and didn't want to enter that curse of codependency yet again. I had a doctors appointment and they scheduled for me to come back the next morning. I was going to be induced.

When I was induced I had an epidural . I wanted to have the epidural right away. I was afraid of what the pain would feel like. I was good at suppressing emotional pain but when it came to physical it would inflict a sense of fear. I'd read all these horror stories on labor and delivery that it kind messed with me. I was nervous about everything. I never experienced any contractions because I was induced. My Hugh functioning anxiety got the best of me and before I knew it my pregnancy was over. I was silent and calm during the delivery. It was a very peaceful moment for me. I didn't have any of my family in the room with me. It was just me and Noelle's dad. Looking back I do sort of regret not having my family present. Would it of made us closer if I did? Would my mom get a chance to be there for me by my side in one of life's memorable moments had I just let her?

A week later I went back to work. I continued waitressing at a local restaurant. I knew I wanted to give my daughter the best future possible. I didn't want her to grow up in a household like I did. I wanted to give her the best life possible anyway I could. I was very grateful to have my family supporting my decisions. It was a great way for me to re-establish bonds with my family. It was an opportunity for my mom and I to continue to repair our relationship. My mom was very hands on with helping me take care of Noelle. My mom immediately began to bond with Noelle. Their bond was formed early. It's a bond that I don't have with my mom.

I began to work six days a week. Within six months or less the man I thought I knew and loved left the household. He was going through some personal problems. Problems that he needed to handle on his own. His absence put me in a position to pick up the slack. I began working late nights and double shifts at the restaurant. It was challenging because I wasn't breastfeeding at the time. So I would have to get up in the middle of the night to make formula.

Being up with Noelle late at night and trying to tend to her needs was hard for me mentally and physically. I was sleep deprived frequently. Work was physically draining. We lived in an apartment alone. Being in a physically demanding industry was not easy on my body. Most people in the apartment community worked 9-5 jobs. So, they took up most of the parking spaces. Which forced me to park further away from the apartment.

I would have to carry Noelle on my hip and any bags on the other hand. Sometimes it would be pitch black and I would have to carry my purse, food from work, and a few other things. It was in these moments that I realized my life was not just about me anymore. My decisions were not about what made me feel good. Everything was about making the tough and uncomfortable decisions to make a better life for Noelle.

Noelle, was my purpose. She gave me purpose and reasons to get up early every morning. She inspired me to keep going know matter how tired I felt each day. It was all for the greater good of giving Noelle a better life than I had. I knew there were sacrifices and risks that needed to be made. I was willing to do whatever it took to give my daughter the best life possible.I promised myself that I would do whatever it took to have a good relationship with my daughter. I promised myself that I would be an amazing mother. I strived to give my daughter the bond I wished I had with my mother.

There were more tough days than easier days raising my daughter alone. Everything fell on my shoulders. My income alone was supporting us. I didn't see this coming yet all my early trials and tribulations in life would prepare me for it. I told myself I will never fail, I could never fail the one who now needed me most. I remember buying a crib for Noelle's room. She rarely slept in her crib because I wanted her next to me. Night time was our special time together. This was the time that we would be able to get together. This was our bonding time. This was also the time I would write in my journal about being financially stable. I wrote about all the things I can do to save money or make more money. I began using coupons to become more frugal. I realized early that my dreams of being a homeowner required me to make a sacrifice and be disciplined with my money. Being single motivated me not to settle for less than I deserved.

Even though I lived in an apartment I knew my goal was to buy a house in a few years. I knew I needed to create a safe and loving environment for me and my daughter. There was one incident where a man dressed in a hoodie jumped onto my balcony. He tried to open the slider glass door. He was attempting to break in. It was a very terrifying moment. I had just resigned my lease for the apartment. Police came checked for prints, questioned neighbors and looked for surrounding footage. That moment in life made me very uncomfortable because I would come home late at night. My home was no longer a home, we weren't safe. We could never go back. Being a single mom I stayed with my mom and realized that apartment was no longer home anymore. Noelle's safety and security was a priority for me. I stayed wth my mom and saved as much money as I could for us. I began going house hunting. I located a two bedroom townhouse. One morning while Noelle was in school I met with a realtor. The townhouse was located a few blocks from my mom. It wasn't on the market yet. As soon as I walked inside I knew it was the perfect home for me and my daughter. It was where I wanted to be, it was my home. I completed the loan and worked hard to remove any debt from my background. It was a long road to repairing my credit. I managed to pay off medical bills etc. to repair my credit. I never realized how important good credit was to my future. I learned early on that a three digit number would be the financial footprint to my success.

Even though I was on the road of recovery and building a solid foundation for my daughter. I still struggled frequently with making enough time for her in my life. As much as I work and make sacrifices to take care of my daughter. I always want to give my daughter the love of a two parent household. I always want to be able to give Noelle anything that she wants in life. She deserves the best from me. Just being able to give her my all and provide a stable upcoming was important to me.After three years of hard work and consistency, it all paid off. We now have a place to call home.

Now, we have a routine of going to church on Sunday and reading together on Monday nights. Anything that can help create a bond between me and my daughter, I do it.

Noelle's father and I haven't been the best at co-parenting. I never forgave him. It wasn't until his recent diagnosis that we have established a bond. Even though he hasn't been actively involved with the upbringing of our daughter, I still have love for him. I never wanted to come in between my daughter having a relationship with her dad. Despite the past I've learned that people make mistakes. People will disappoint you and let you down in life. It's up to you to keep going and figure out the life you want to create for yourself. Our love for our daughter would always out rule any obstacle.

Part II

Chapter Twelve
Before You Can Go Forward, You Must Look Back

When I look back over my life, I'm reminded of how far and how much I've overcome. When people look at me they admire me for my strength, courage, and drive. As much as I admire their kind words , it's not a loss for me the things I had to sacrifice to get where I am. I never realized how much I was giving up to be where I am today. For most of my life I've struggled to feel comfortable within my skin. I fought many battles to find a place of peace and comfort. It was tough making decisions for myself. I always strived to be at a place where I could thrive and grow simultaneously. Though has often revealed to be you don't always get the result you desire. You get the result of your choices and sacrifices. I

learned that when I was searching for a piece of myself that I lost in my childhood. There was a growing gap in the woman I often presented to the world. I was attempting to push past all of the trauma and confusion that were established in my life. Even though I didn't have much of a choice in my upbringing. I wanted to give myself the life I deserved as an adult. Sometimes, I didn't get it right. Sometimes I hurt more people than I intended too. Sometimes I lost more of myself trying to appease others. Through it all I learned to find the inner strength to face life obstacles and keep going. Maybe I learned this mentality from watching my mother work long hours and sacrifice her dreams for the sake of her children. It was hard for me to understand her choices as a child. But, as a woman I understand that the tough decisions are the ones that build character.

The resentment that I began to carry around with me from childhood to adulthood blocked me from receiving many blessings. The most valuable thing we don't own is time. I wished that I could go back in a moment in time and forgive my dad sooner. Forgiveness is not easy for me. But, I know that I will always regret not having more time with my dad. I realize people don't live forever. I hoped that we had more time to resolve our differences. I wished that my dad understood where I was coming from and all of the things I was battling silently. So often I allowed people to assume their own assumptions of me. It didn't matter to others that I was hurting on the inside and filled with turmoil, chaos, and pain. I just wanted to be loved and accepted by those around me. When I couldn't find hope or relief from my family I chose a more destructive path. A path that would ultimately test my will to keep living, the love of my family, and my search for purpose. I knew I caused my family more scrife and headaches at times. That was never my intention. I was on a path of trying to discover my purpose and unlearn everything I'd been told about life. I discovered that I was not alone in my suffering to build a better life. I just went about things a different way than other people. I lost my way quite a few times by associating with the wrong people. I don't look back at my life with regret or shame. I understand that I had to find my way the best way I knew how at the time. My choices did cost me time with my family and time with my dad. That will always haunt me as long as I live. But, I've learned not to dwell on the things I can no longer change. The past has taught me that I can overcome the worst challenges and live to fight another day.

There were days where I found it tough to get out of bed in the morning. There were times where I thought getting high was all that mattered in the world. It was my escape from my reality. When I would come down from my high life would smack me in the face hard. I soon realized after some time that life was not about getting high or running away from your problems. Life is about facing the hardships and uncomfortable moments with courage and faith.

I didn't grow up in a religious household. I knew God existed. I had a more spiritual relationship with God. I knew God was real because I would often pray for clarity and guidance. Guidance to get me closer to Him and find peace in my life. I would often talk to God in my quiet moments. I was always nervous to pray or speak to him for quite some time. The thought of was I deserving enough or were my acts deemed unforgivable as I would thought to be casted to hell always crossed my mind. I was scared to pray. Would praying conjure some demonic obstacles along my path to have me bare my sorrow? Speaking to my sister in years to come would change all forgoing thoughts and crush all hesitation I feared. It was there that I knew I could talk openly and honestly with Him. My prayers would always be answered in just the nick of time. I am beyond grateful for my relationship with God. Without God I don't know how I would have ever made it to where I am today.

When people ask me what I'm most excited about in the next stage of my life, it's the future. The future used to scare me growing up because of our household. There were days where my heart would race rapidly. I could hardly sleep through the night or focus in school. Tomorrow always seemed so far away. I didn't know what the future held for me. I didn't know how I would make it to see one birthday after the next. Today, my heart is filled with hope and promise. I've learned from my poor decisions and life challenges. I'm in a place of peace and happiness. Everything is not perfect and I've learned they will never be perfect. That's quite alright with me because I have so much more to look forward to. I'm grateful for my circle of family and friends. They inspire me to keep going and aspire to become my greater self. They refuse to allow me to give up on myself to settle for less than I deserve. If life has shown me anything it's that I am a fighter . I'll always fight to live in peace and harmony. Fight to give my children a better life than I had growing up. Fight for more time to be with the people we love and cherish the most.

My family is my rock and my center when I feel down on myself. They've held me close and continue to push me towards pursuing my goals. I've always wanted to live a life that inspires other women to pursue their goals. It doesn't matter what challenges you face in this life, you have the power to change it.

Life will continuously knock you down and tell you to give up. Don't let it! You have to find the inner strength to push past your circumstances and fight for your future. Everyday will not be tough, hard, or difficult to handle. There will be good days where things will work in your favor. You have to trust and believe that your life has purpose. There are people counting on you to win. Win so that you can uplift the next person behind you. There is someone in your life looking at you with hope and promise to keep going. They need to see you win, to give them hope to win in their lives. Don't dwell on your failures and shortcomings. Life happens to all of us. For all the times I thought my life was over, God gave me a new beginning. I thought my bad choices would follow me for the rest of my life. People counted me out early because of my upbringing. No one expected me to make anything out of my life. I almost believed them. Sometimes God will use our friends and family to wake us up. He'll demand we pay closer attention to what He has called us to do here on earth. I was lost for the longest time. That is until God saved me. He saved me from myself. He gave me a reason to keep fighting for a better tomorrow. I want to encourage you to live and fight for brighter days ahead. It doesn't matter what you've been through in this life. You have fought long and hard to get to where your life's worth living. You will survive the test of all your bad days and be victorious in the end. Trust me, if I can do it, so can you. I went through the toughest obstacles of my life alone. I thought God had forgotten about me when I was going through my challenges. He was with me all along. We may face the worst of the worst life challenges in our lifetime. Those challenges make us stronger and more resilient for where God is trying to take us. Be prepared for a bumpy ride along the way. Sometimes we want God to answer our prayers without experiencing the hardship of life. The battles will not destroy, they will make us appreciate our relationship with God. Our faith is our guiding force to overcoming the many obstacles that will come in our direction. Know matter how it may look on the outside, God will always be present.

As long as we can live to fight another day, we can conquer anything.

Chapter Thirteen
Understanding Your Financial Independence

I understood early on in my adult life the importance of being financially independent. When I left my dad's house I understood that making my own money was key to my independence. Earning my own money meant that I could control my freedom and my life. I knew that going back to my dad's house was not the best option for me. There was nothing left for me at my dad's house besides confusion and chaos. I realized early that I needed to develop some healthy habits about money. Habits that would allow me to be stable and financially independent.

From an early age I realized that my father was the breadwinner in our household. Even though my mother was a contributor in our upbringing raising the children. She was limited in how far she could go when it was time to start over. I never wanted to be put into a situation where I didn't have the power to come and go as I pleased in my life. I knew from an early age money was an essential resource. Whether we had a little or not, it was a pivotal key in establishing the sort of lifestyle I wanted to maintain. I realized that my mother came from a different generation of women who made the tough decision to stay home. I can respect her tough choices to provide a stable and warm home for us. But, I can't help but wonder about the tough decisions she had to make in her own life. How would her life have been different if she made her own money before the divorce? As a woman, I knew I always wanted to position myself to be in control of my life. Money gave me that option.

Whether you are a single mom or college student, you need to understand the importance of being financially independent. Yes, relationships are great. Having a partner that compliments your effort is a bonus in your book. I want to talk more in depth about identifying ways to make your money work for you long term.

Women have a lot more challenges when it comes to earning money. We often receive less than our male counterparts. We have to address the "glass ceiling" , the unseen barrier in the workplace. The glass ceiling prevents women from receiving promotions and career advancements. In addition to the fact that as women a greater portion of our lives are spent raising children.

When we choose to have children it's a sacrifice. It's a personal choice to stop and begin to grow our families. The drawback is we spend less time in the workplace and earn less income. We love our children and value building a family with our partners. However, women are tasked with losing out on advancing their careers. This can often be discouraging and challenging when you are a thought leader in your industry. Don't get me wrong children are precious and worth the sacrifice. Women should not have to choose between raising a family or advancing in the workplace.

Unfortunately, it's a choice that we make on a daily basis in the United States.

Another valid point is that women are often the caretakers of their respective families. When the elders in our families are no longer able to care for themselves. Women usually are tasks with the responsibility of being caretakers and providers. This is ultimately a drain on the body, spirit, and your bank account. This isn't to say that men aren't capable of being caretakers of the elders. However, the role usually falls on the laps of women who are the nurturers of the family. As a result of trying to wear multiple hats for those in the family we love and care about. We hold ourselves hostage in advancing our careers.

All of these are valid examples of where women are sacrificing their income and independence. Women often do maintain regular jobs throughout their lifetimes. However, a lot of time and money is lost when women don't acquire the skills to invest, save , and prepare to accumulate wealth.

Becoming financially independent is not just a trending hashtag on social media. It's a necessity for women everywhere. I want to help you secure your family's financial future, cut household expenses, live in peace, and live a rewarding life you don't need a vacation from.

So what are the steps to financial independence? Keep reading to find out!

Step I: Identify What You Want

As women the world has told us that all we want are diamonds and pointy expensive high heeled shoes to match. Not quite. As women, we have the power to make our own decisions. Whether you come from a family of traumatic experiences or a middle class family. You have the power to decide what sort of life you want to live. What decisions are those? Ask yourself these questions :

1.   What am I striving to accomplish at this stage in my life? What skills have I obtained to make me money? What skills do I need to have more earning potential?

2.   What do I value most in my life today? What am I teaching my children about money? Am I saving more than I'm spending?

3.   What am I willing to sacrifice to get to where I want to be? What am I afraid of losing the most?

4.   What are my goals? How will I work towards those goals today?

The answers to these questions determine what decisions you need to make. Think of it like you're creating a road map for your life. Yes, it's going to be some detours, delays, and obstacles along the way. But, this roadmap is your guide and commitment to creating the life you want for yourself. That destination will empower you to keep going when the road gets tough. You will have something that you are working towards. You're on the road of self fulfillment. You will pack all of the supplies and tools you need to get to where you're going in life. Don't be scared or fearful of change. This is what you said you wanted for yourself. You owe it to yourself to see your dreams coming true. The first step to becoming financially independent is choosing your own life's path.

You're right. Choosing a destination can be a bit intimidating to think about. Afterall you're stepping outside of your comfort zone to achieve what seemed impossible. It's natural to feel a little nervous, I was once nervous too. Can I tell you something? Not choosing a destination for my life was more terrifying than anything. I wanted everything I could imagine with my mind. I held on to those moments where I could travel with my family. I held on to the memory of what it was like to see more than enough money in my account. I want you to know that your dreams are possible. A life of financial freedom and independence is all within reach. The first step is identify what you want and how you're going to get there. Don't accept nothing less than you deserve.

Step 2 : Own Your Cash Flow

You know what you want and how you plan on getting there. Now, let's focus on your cash flow. It's important to identify how you're going to take care of yourself long after your working years. For example, maybe you want to retire in the next few years. Perhaps you'd like to live abroad and live modestly. Whatever you decide, you need to make sure you're in a position to live comfortably. How are you going to do that?

Lets identify what cash flow is and how you're going to keep it coming in. Cash flow is the amount of money you have coming in and going out. Thus, it's important to note whether or not you have more money going out than you do coming in, you have a big problem. This can hinder you from reaching your goals and certainly securing your financially independent future. The last thing you want looming over your head is debt. Debt is not sexy and will definitely put a monkey wrench in your future plans. Not getting your debt under control is a risk women can't take. When it comes to controlling your cash flow, you will need to keep a few things in mind.

They are your income and your expenses.

As a golden rule of finance, you cannot be financially independent unless your income is more than your expenses. Sounds right? Good.

Unfortunately, most people don't have a financial game plan of how they're going to get by in their retirement years. Luckily, that's not you! You're taking the steps to have cash flow coming in when you retire.

Cash flow is beyond being in a position to pay your bills. Your roadmap to where you want to be in the next five or ten years will cost you money. Thus, in order for you to control your cash flow, you'll need to start calculating your expected income and expenses. Let's break this down a

little further for more clarity.

- What is your monthly income after taxes?
- How much do you pay in monthly utilities?
- How much debt do you have, and what are your monthly payments?
- How much do you spend on auto insurance, life, home, and gas? Do you have any outer pocket expenses?

Now, let's begin running the numbers by subtracting your expenses from your income. Whatever number you get is what you have available to put toward your financial goals. This is your current cash flow. What about your expected cash flow? Your expenses are likely to change after retirement. Thus your expenses could go up significantly after you retire. Hopefully this is ringing a few bells for you.

The truth is no one knows what the future may hold especially financially. We do agree that it's important to prepare for the storm before it rains. We all have a mass debt throughout our lifetimes through college or credit cards. You're not alone. The important thing is to remember that you need a plan to eliminate your debt and become financially independent in the future.

Step 3: Say Goodbye To Your Debt

Debt is such an ugly word. It's something you don't want to take into a marriage or pass down to your kids. Your debt will follow you for the rest of your life. Know matter how far you try to out run it, it will show up with bells on. So , what's the best course of action? Deal with it.

You're not alone in tackling your debt. People who work in high profile positions are working through their loads of debt. The only difference between them and you is the method of how you are handling it. Women tend to have more debt than men.

Why? Think about it. We go to the doctor more than men, elective surgeries to our bodies, shopping habits, and etc.

Largely, women debt out in part to unequal pay to our male counterparts. Just like men, many women take on student loans or mortgages and spend more than they can afford. Thus tackling your debt is critical for having the financial independent future you dream. Ready to tackle your debt?

Here are a few pointers:

1.	Establish healthy habits early on: Before you answer an ad for debt consolidation give this a shot. Identifying your habits that got you into debt in the first place. I've been guilty of splurging over the weekend with my girlfriends. I'm guilty for swiping my credit card outside of emergencies. In the end , those things come back and bite you and me. Unfortunately, we live in a society that promotes living a materialistic lifestyle. Your status on social media goes up when you post the latest designer threads or a new car. We all deserve nice things. However, everything has its place and time in your life. If you know you can't afford it or don't need it to survive, leave it. It's easy to get in debt. It's hard to break the habits that got you into it. Put yourself on a budget each month. You should be saving more than you are spending. If you are able to do that, you're heading in the right direction.

2.	Budgeting is key to a financial future : We briefly talked about a budget above. Let's go a little bit deeper and kill two birds with one stone. You understand the value of money. When you know better, you can do better. Creating a budget is always a good idea. Having a budget is essential to your financial future. It's sort of like having a screen protector over your phone but for your financial future. When you establish a budget, you empower yourself to make better decisions around your money. Your budget will give you the insight you need to prepare for an unexpected event. Budgeting allows you to allocate all of your money and have some saved for the future. It means that you get to determine exactly how much you save each month. You're being mindful of what you spend your money on and where it's spent. Budgeting gives you more control over your money.

3.	Consider paying off higher debts first: Think about your largest debt to date. Would you rather pay the highest debt off first or work your way towards it? Most people would rather pay off their biggest debt first. It just makes more common sense.

There's nothing wrong with paying off your smaller debts first. However, if you focus on the larger debt amount, you will pay out less in interest and tasks won't seem too overwhelming. Have you ever tried paying for something and didn't feel as if you were making progress? The same feeling will consume you if you pay the small debts off first. It's important to be strategic and begin to effectively decrease your debts.

Step 4: Earn, Save, and Invest

Maybe your girlfriends have talked to you about investing your money. Maybe it was a infomercial late at night. Either way, you've heard the words invest a few times before. Investing is making your money work for you, you do not have to work for it. Makes sense? Hopefully so. For most of your adult life, you've worked long hours to earn your money. At some point, you'll be ready to kick back and relax. You won't be a spring chicken anymore. Thus, you'll need to make some wise decisions in advance to enjoy the fruits of your labor.

Saving your money for a rainy day is not the same as investing your money. Saving your money is imperative. For example, when the pandemic hit us all unexpectedly. Were you able to pay your bills and rent consistently? Were you eager to anticipate a pay out from the government?

Most people were not prepared financially for the unexpected events of 2020. Life always gives us unexpected moments to teach us the hard lessons. Having a financial game plan is key to pivoting forward. You always want to position yourself to be able to self -sufficient for three to six months. As a golden rule, if you save your money, your money will be able to save you.

Hopefully you can take my advice and make the best choices possible to have a financially independent life. Your life will always give you opportunities to move one step closer towards your dreams. Take every chance to live the life you always imagined. If I can do it so can you.

Chapter Fourteen
Your Faith Can Move Mountains

There was a time in my life where I didn't know if I would live to see today. I made some questionable choices that scared my family. If it wasn't for my faith in God, I wouldn't be here today. When I was going through the toughest periods of my life I found it difficult to keep going. You may can relate to where I once was in my life. Life took me through a lot of ups and downs. The downs caused me to question my will to live and move forward. I didn't grow up in a household where we went to church throughout the week. What I did have were people in my life that continuously prayed for me. Prayed for me when I didn't know how to pray for myself. God surrounded me with people who were able to love me beyond my obstacles. I am the product of my grandparents prayers. My mom and siblings pray too. When I was at my darkest there prayers covered me. I'm grateful for all those people who loved me despite my many setbacks in life. If you're facing challenges in your life, I want you to remember a few things:

I.   Prayer changes everything: I used to talk to God about the things I was carrying on the inside of me. I didn't know the perfect prayer or scripture. I just began to speak openly from my heart. God listened to me when I was crying my eyes out. God heard me when I was asking for Him to save me. When I felt like I didn't have anyone, God was right by my side. Prayer is not about saying the right things for God to save you. Prayer is about being open and vulnerable to allow God inside your heart. Trust in God with everything that you are facing. He understands more than you know. He can save you from your burdens and give you a new beginning.

2.   Forgive people for yourself : I don't think I will ever forget the pain and trauma growing up. It's embedded inside of my brain. My father was not a perfect man. He was a man filled with flaws and battles of his own. I may never understand the reasons why he chose to drink or become verbally abusive towards us. I know I will never get the apology I deserve from him. I've come to understand that there is power in forgiveness. I forgive my father for causing me so much pain and loss of my childhood. I forgive my dad for not being able to love me the way I deserved to be loved. I forgive my dad for passing down his brokenness to me.

I forgive my dad for not being able to out live his illness to see where I am today. I forgive my dad for everything because he didn't know the pain he would cause me for a lifetime. I've learned that forgiveness is not for the other person. It's for me. I can now look back on my life and be grateful. I'm grateful for being able to outgrow the challenges that were meant to destroy me.

3.   Keep living, there's more life to live: Getting high and running away from my problems used to be my outlet. I used to crave that feeling because I thought I needed it to live. I don't. That feeling was just to numb me from dealing with my reality. Today, I've found hope and purpose in finding light in being with my family. Everyday isn't perfect. But, I've found purpose in everyday life. You can too. You're not your mistakes. You're not the person that people think you are in their heads. You're the person you decide to be everyday you choose to fight to live.

4.   Express gratitude often : When was the last time you expressed thanks for just being alive? I lost my dad. It hurt my heart tremendously because we ran out of time. If I could go back and have one more conversation. It wouldn't be to talk about whose right and whose wrong. It would just to say thank you. As a parent, I understand now that God puts people in our

lives for a reason. Those people may not be perfect. But, there the people we get to share this journey of life.beside. Everyday I write down at least ten things I'm grateful for in my life. It doesn't matter if they are big or small, I'm grateful to have them. Before you complain about the things you don't have or wish you had. Take a good look around and give thanks for the things you do have in your life.

5.   Believe In You: I'll always hold close to my heart the times that I was able to make my mom proud of me. I'll always remember the way he her eyes would light up when she saw me on stage. It was like she saw a part of herself inside of me. I lived a great part of my life trying to make other people proud of me. I know that the people I love will always mean well. But, I needed to believe in me just as much as they did. I don't live in regret. But, I often think about the road I didn't take and where would I be today. I didn't have a lot of belief in myself back then. I was busy trying to figure things out as I grew older. Even though I didn't get a chance to explore all of my dreams. I found the strength to believe in myself to accomplish anything. Sometimes you will have to be your loudest cheerleader. Sometimes your family won't support all of your decisions. Sometimes you're going to make some bad choices.

Sometimes you'll have to go through the worst in order to appreciate the good. I'm proud of myself because I found the courage to believe in a bigger and brighter tomorrow.

6.   Starting Over Is Not Easy : I started over in a new city and state to be closer to my family. There was something greater waiting for me on the other side of the country. Even though I had supportive friends in California, it couldn't replace my family. Maybe you're in a similar place in your life. My advice is to take a risk and bet on yourself. Don't allow fear to rule your life. Fear will keep you stuck and heading down a dark path. Starting over doesn't mean that you are a failure. It takes courage to start over and try something new. Most people go there entire lives never taking a chance. They live in regret and wish they would have moved on to better things. Don't allow where you come from or life challenges to keep you stuck. You deserve to see the world for all it has to offer. Don't settle for good enough when you can have greater.

7.   You owe yourself no apologies: Even though I would not wish my life choices on anyone. I don't live in regret of my decisions. Everything I went through made me stronger and wiser today. I never want to regret what I thought was best for me at that

time. I didn't understand myself or life as much as I thought. It was all apart of God plan to get my attention and teach me life lessons. Life lessons don't always come perfectly packaged in a bow. Sometimes they come dressed up in a pile of hot mess for you to figure out along the way. Don't beat yourself up for not having it all figured out at your age. No one has it all figured out. What we have figured out is that it takes one day at a time to make it through life.

In order to live you must go through a few things. Some of those things will give you scars and wounds. Others will give you nightmares and spark beautiful dreams. Know matter what you go through in this life, keep God in the middle. God saved me from myself and He'll do the same for you. You don't have to be defined by your past. You have the power to create a future for yourself. You just have to find the strength to start anew.

Chapter Fifteen
Overcoming Codependency: The Importance Of Becoming Your Own Best Friend

When I was searching for love, I found myself codependent on the men in my life. They were often void fillers for me. A lot of our time spent together was more about me filling in the gaps of my childhood. I hated being alone. Alone was a scary place for me. Part of the reason is because I could hear my father's voice inside my head. His negative and verbally abusive tone would play loudly on repeat. It was a constant reminder for me to prove my father wrong. I was more than just a troubled kid that no one understood. I was worthy of the love my parents could not easily provide in many ways. The men I chose were supposed to replace the negative feelings I had about men in my life. They were supposed to make me forget the pain and the wounds of the scars I wore on my sleeve. Instead the men only reopened old wounds and caused me to bleed. For years, I would often wonder to myself how was I going to get out of the cycle of bad relationships. One after the other I discovered that relationships were more than just about being in a relationships. Relationships required vulnerability, compromise, and emotional maturity. I wasn't quite ready. I allowed my partners to lead me blindly in a lot of ways. This ultimately led me to be codependent on men.

There were times where I realized that the men in my life were bad for me. There was no future with most of them. I knew that early on in some relationships. But, I denied my instincts and remained. I stayed because I didn't want to fill the void of a cold bed. Or not having someone to occasionally talk too drove me crazy. I was hurting myself and asking for the pain to continue.

I knew I wanted better for myself. I didn't know the exact steps to take to break away. I always had my own money. I always knew how to recover from my mistakes. But,I was running from my broken relationship with my father. The more I tried to run, hide, or ignore it, the void of not talking to my father had a impact on me. It wasn't until I grew older that I would continue to attract men similar to my father.

Until I began to seek the love I was needing from others from myself.

I began to heal. I began to become my own best friend.

It was not easy in the beginning. It was challenging because I was comfortable being in a relationship. Having the support of another person worked better for me. But, I needed to grow outside of my comfort zone and really get to know myself. I started spending more time alone and doing things that made me happy. I learned that my happiness was not tied to a relationship. It was in the little or small things I did to create happiness for myself. I went back to the basics of what I needed to thrive in the world. For the longest time I was operating on the old version of the young girl I used to be. I was ready to bloom into the woman God called me to be.

As a woman , it's important to establish your own identity before you enter into a relationship. Too often we enter relationships to create stability, love, and commitment. But, somehow we also lean more into what the demands of the relationship require of us. We become codependent on our partners to lead. That's not the way it's supposed to be. A relationship is supposed to add to your happiness.Before you jump into a relationship be clear on who you are first and where you are in your life. If you're not happy with your life, be single. Take your time to become your own best friend. At the end of the day, you'll be there for yourself long after the relationship is over. Don't abandon your hopes, dreams, and goals for anyone. Commit to living your best life. The right man will come along and will want to help advance your life forward.

Never settle. People will always come in and out of your life. They will try to throw you off course or give you less than you deserve. Don't accept it. You deserve the world and all it has to offer.If you don't have all of what your hearts desire keep working towards. You get it eventually.

Surround yourself with women who have bigger and bolder dreams than you do. I know we all think the next woman is our competition. She's not. The next woman is trying to make it just like you. Why not collaborate? We are always stronger together than we are apart. No one makes it to the alone. Women can relate to where you've been and give you tips and insight to get where you are going. Don't judge another woman's story unless you've walked in it.

The road to loving yourself is not easy. It's going to be long, hard, and filled with many detours and delays. I promise you if you keep pushing towards what you want, you'll get to your destination. Every obstacle you are facing right now in your life is set to test your limits. It's not going to break you because you are unbreakable. Your spirit is one of a warrior and a goddess. Believe in yourself and trust the process of getting to where you want to be someday. If I can make it happen for myself, I know you can too.

Chapter Sixteen
Lesson Learned

When I first began writing this book I was nervous and scared. I was scared of what people would think about me. I almost talked myself out of writing about my childhood. I didn't want to be judged. I didn't want my family looking at me sideways. I didn't want to relive the tough moments of my childhood. I didn't want to be another writer with a sad story to share. Then, I had a lightbulb moment where God spoke to me loud and clearly. He told me it was time to heal. It was time for me to face the future and release the past. I was holding on to the experiences in my life that I thought would make or break me.

Those experiences were slowing me down and blocking my future.

I promised myself that I would be as open and transparent as possible. I wanted to shed the burdens of growing up in a dysfunctional household. I know the people in my life may not understand the reason for writing the book. Deep down I prayed that a book like this would fall into my arms when I needed the words and wisdom the most. Long behold I would be the one to write the words and not be the reader hoping for the message. Some people may never forgive me for living in my truth. But, it's my truth. It's my experience that I needed to share with the world. I regret nothing because I've been through enough to know life gets better. How I choose to live my life is entirely up to me.

This book is a vivid reminder that you can go through the worst and still make a life. People counted me out early on in my life. They said I would never amount to anything. They said I would become another statistic. They said I deserved whatever hand life dealt me because I was ungrateful and selfish. I'm so glad I didn't listen to those people. I found the courage to keep living. As many times as I have fallen, I found the strength to get up and fight again.

www.ingramcontent.com/pod-product-compliance
Lightning Source LLC
Chambersburg PA
CBHW040812120726

48005CB00012B/1399